The Path of Freedom

Henri J. M. Nouwen

The Path of Freedom

CROSSROAD • NEW YORK

1995

The Crossroad Publishing Company
370 Lexington Avenue, New York, NY 10017

Printed in the United States of America

ISBN 0-8245-2001-7

THIS LITTLE BOOK is a story about an accident...my own. When I was hit by a van while hitchhiking and rushed to the emergency room of the nearby hospital, I found myself suddenly at the portal of death. Since I did not die, but returned to good health, I am able to tell my story. I now dare to say that this interruption gave me a new knowledge of God. And so, more strongly than ever, I feel a need to write about it and simply present this knowledge that I cannot keep for myself alone.

I hope and pray that this glimpse beyond the mirror will bring comfort and hope to my brothers and sisters who are afraid to think of their approaching death, or who think of it in fear and trembling.

The Accident

Two vivid recollections remain in me of that moment on a dark winter morning when the outside rearview mirror of a passing van struck me in the back and flung me to the ground beside the road. I knew at once that I had reached a point of no return.

As I lay by the side of the busy road, crying for help, I knew also from the instant I was hit that this was not purely an accident. Later I would be able to see clearly how predictable, providential, and mysteriously planned the whole event was. At the time, my primary concern was that help would arrive, yet I realized that something strangely "good" was happening on the side of the road.

As I lay there, I tried to shout and wave to the two attendants of a nearby gas station, but they were too far off either to see or hear me. Then, to my surprise, a young man came running toward me. He bent over me and said, "Let me help you, you've been hurt!" His voice was very gentle and friendly. He seemed like a protecting angel. "A passing car must have hit me," I said. "I don't even know if the driver noticed." "It was me," he replied. "I hit you with my right mirror, and I stopped to help you. . . . Can you stand up?" "Yes, I guess I can," I said, and with his help, I got on my feet. "Be careful," he cautioned, "be very careful." Together we walked toward the gas station. "My name is Henri," I said. "I'm Jon," he answered. "Let me try to get you an ambulance." We entered the gas station, and Jon put me in a chair and grabbed the phone. The two attendants looked on from a distance but said nothing. After a minute, Jon grew impatient. "I can't get through to the ambulance service. I had better take you to the hospital myself."

Looking out of the door window, I saw the twisted mirror and realized how hard I had been hit. Jon was obviously shaken. He asked, "Why where you standing along the road?" I didn't want to explain too much but said, "I am a priest living in a community with mentally handicapped people, and I was on my way to work in one of our houses." With noticeable consternation in his voice, he said, "Oh, my God, I hit a priest. Oh, my God." I tried to console him: "I am really grateful to you for taking me to the hospital, and when I am better, you must come to visit our community." "Yes, I'd like to," he said, but his thoughts were elsewhere.

The Hospital

As soon as we reached the emergency room of the hospital, we were surrounded by nurses, doctors, a policewoman, questions and answers, admission forms, and X-rays. People were extremely friendly, efficient, competent, and straightforward. The doctor who looked at the X-rays said, "You've broken five ribs. We'll keep you here for a day and then let you go home." Then, unexpectedly, a very familiar face appeared. It was my G.P., Dr. Prasad. I was surprised at how quickly she had come. Seeing her gave me a deep sense of being in good hands. But at that very moment I started to feel terribly sick. I became quite dizzy and wanted to vomit, but couldn't. I noticed some consternation around me, and within a few minutes it became clear that I was a lot worse off than I had thought. "There is some internal bleeding going on," said Dr. Prasad. "We must keep a close watch on you."

After many tests, tubes, and talks, I learned that the internal damage was critical and severe. I was taken to the intensive-care unit. Now I was able to let the truth sink in. I was very sick and even in danger of losing my life. Faced with the possibility of dying, it came to me that the mirror of the passing van had forced me to look at myself in a radically new way.

Except for brief, insignificant ill-nesses, I had never been in a hospital bed. But now, suddenly, I had become a real patient, totally dependent on the people around me. I could do nothing without help. The tubes going into my body at different places for intravenous injections, blood transfusions, and heart monitoring were evidence that I had become truly "passive."

Knowing my very impatient disposition and aware of my need to stay in control, I expected this new situation to be extremely frustrating. But the opposite occurred. I felt quite safe in my hospital bed with its railings on both sides. Notwithstanding the severe pain, I had a completely unexpected sense of security. The doctors and nurses explained every move they made, gave me the name of each medicine they injected, warned me beforehand of upcoming pain, and expressed their confidence as well as their doubts about the effects of their actions.

The Surgery

On Friday morning, after many more tests, Dr. Barnes, the surgeon, said, "Your spleen is still bleeding. We have to take it out." "When?" I asked, and he said, "As soon as the operating room is free." A little later Dr. Prasad came to see me. Again I felt the threat of death. She was very honest and told me all she knew. I myself felt that dying was quite possible and that I had to prepare myself and my friends for it. Somewhere, deep in me, I sensed that my life was in real danger. And so I let myself enter into a place I had never been before: the portal of death. I wanted to know that place, to "walk around" it, and make myself ready for a life beyond life.

It was the first time in my life that I consciously walked into this seemingly fearful place, the first time I looked forward to what might be a new way of being. I tried to let go of my familiar world, my history, my friends, my plans. I tried not to look back, but ahead. I kept looking at that door that might open to me and show me something beyond anything I had ever seen.

What I experienced then was something I had never experienced before: pure and unconditional love. Better still, what I experienced was an intensely personal presence, a presence that pushed all my fears aside and said: "Come, don't be afraid. I love you"; a very gentle, nonjudgmental presence; a presence that simply asked me to trust and trust completely. It was not a warm light, a rainbow, or an open door that I *saw,* but a human yet divine presence that I *felt,* inviting me to come closer and to let go of all fears.

My whole life had been an arduous attempt to follow Jesus as I had come to know him through my parents, friends, and teachers. I had spent countless hours studying the Scriptures, listening to lectures and sermons, and reading spiritual books. Jesus had been very close to me, but also very distant; a friend, but also a stranger; a source of hope, but also of fear, guilt, and shame. But now, when I walked in the portal of death, all ambiguity and all uncertainty were gone. He was there, the Lord of my life, saying, "Come to me, come."

Death lost its power and shrank away in the Life and Love that surrounded me in such an intimate way, as if I were walking through a sea whose waves were rolled back to create a path for me. I was being held safe while moving toward the other shore. All jealousies, resentments, and angers were being gently moved away, and I was being shown that Love and Life are greater, deeper, and stronger than any of the forces I had been worrying about.

One emotion was very strong —

Death lost its power
and shrank away
in the Life and Love
that surrounded me
in such an intimate way.

that of homecoming. Jesus opened his home to me and seemed to say, "Here is where you belong." The words he spoke to his disciples — "In my Father's house there are many places to live in...I am going now to prepare a place for you" (John 14:2) — became very real. The risen Jesus, who now dwells with his Father, was welcoming me home after a long journey.

This experience was the realization of my oldest and deepest desires. Since the first moment of consciousness, I have had the desire to be with Jesus. Now I felt his presence in a most tangible way, as if my whole life had come together and I was being enfolded in love. The homecoming had a real quality of return, a return to the womb of

God. The God who had fashioned me in secret and molded me in the depths of the earth, the God who had knitted me together in my mother's womb was calling me back after a long journey and wanted to receive me back as someone who had become child enough to be loved as a child. I speak only for myself here, and I simply trust that I had a very clear vision in the face of death.

Still, there were resistances to the call to come home. I spoke about them to Sue, one of my l'Arche friends, during one of her visits. What most prevented me from dying was the sense of unfinished business, unresolved conflicts with people with whom I live or had lived. The pain of forgiveness withheld, by me and from me, kept me clinging to my wounded existence. In my mind's eye, I saw the men and women who aroused within me feelings of anger, jealousy, and even hatred.

They had a strange power over me. They might never think of me, but every time I thought of them I lost some of my inner peace and joy. Their criticism, rejection, or expressions of personal dislike still affected my feelings about myself. By not truly forgiving them from the heart, I gave them a power over me that kept me chained to my old, broken existence. I also knew that there were still people angry with me, people who could not think about me or speak about me without experiencing great hostility. I might not even know what I had done or said to them. I might not even know who they were. They had not forgiven me but held on to me in their anger.

In the face of death, I realized that it was not love that kept me clinging to life but unresolved anger. Love, real love flowing from me or toward me, sets me free to die. Death would not undo that love. To the contrary, death would deepen it and strengthen it. Those whom I love dearly and those by whom I am loved dearly may mourn my death, but their bonds with me will only grow stronger and deeper. They would remember me, make me part of their very members, and thus carry my spirit with them on their journey.

No, the real struggle was not a matter of leaving loved ones. The real struggle had to do with leaving behind me people whom I had not forgiven and people who had not forgiven me. These feelings kept me bound to the old body and brought me great sadness. I suddenly felt an immense desire to call around my bed all who were angry with me and all with whom I was angry, to embrace them, ask them to forgive me, and offer them my forgiveness.

As I thought of them, I realized that they represented a host of opinions, judgments, and even condemnations that had enslaved me to this world. It almost seemed that much of my energy had gone into proving to myself and to others that I was right in my conviction that some people could not be trusted, that others were using me or were

*"Please tell everyone
who has hurt me
that I forgive them
from my heart,
and please ask everyone
whom I have hurt
to forgive me too."*

trying to push me aside, and that whole groups and categories of people were falling short of the mark. Thus I kept holding on to the illusion that I am destined to be the evaluator and judge of human behavior.

As I felt life weakening in me, I felt a deep desire to forgive and to be forgiven, to let go of all evaluations and opinions, to be free from the burden of judgments. I said to Sue, "Please tell everyone who has hurt me that I forgive them from my heart, and please ask everyone whom I have hurt to forgive me too."

As I said this, I felt I was taking off the wide leather belts that I had worn while chaplain with the rank of captain in the army. Those belts not only

girded my waist, but also crossed my
chest and shoulders. They had given
me prestige and power. They had en-
couraged me to judge people and put
them in their place. Although my stay
in the army was very brief, I had, in
my mind, never fully removed my belts.
But I knew now that I did not want to
die with these belts holding me captive.
I had to die powerless, without belts,
completely free from judgment.

What worried me most during those
hours was that my death might make
someone feel guilty, ashamed, or sus-
pended spiritually in midair. I was
afraid that someone would say or
think, "I wish there had been a chance
to resolve our conflict, to say what I
really feel, to express my true intentions

...I wish, but now it is too late." I know how hard it is to live with these unsaid words and withheld gestures. They can deepen our darkness and become a burden of guilt.

I knew that my dying could be good or bad for others, depending on the choice I made in the face of it. I said again to Sue, "In case I die, tell everyone that I feel an immense love for all the people I have come to know, also toward those with whom I live in conflict. Tell them not to feel anxious or guilty but to let me go into the house of my Father and to trust that there my communion with them will grow deeper and stronger. Tell them to celebrate with me and be grateful for all that God has given me."

That was all I could do. Sue received my words with a very open heart, and I knew that she would let them bear fruit. She looked at me with great gentleness and let me know that all was well. From that moment on I gave myself over to Jesus and felt like a little chick safe under the wings of its mother. That sense of safety had something to do with the consciousness that anguish had come to an end: anguish from not being able to receive the love I wanted to receive, and from not being able to give the love I most wanted to give; anguish caused by feelings of rejection and abandonment.

The blood that I was losing in such quantity became a metaphor for the anguish that had plagued me for so many years. It too would flow out of me, and I would come to know the love that I had yearned for with all my heart. Jesus was there to offer me the love of his Father, a love that I most desired to receive, a love also that would enable me to give all. Jesus himself had lived anguish. He knew the pain of being unable to give or receive what he most valued. But he lived through that anguish with the trust that his Father, who had sent him, would never leave him alone. And now Jesus was there, standing beyond all anguish and calling me to "the other country."

•

When the nurses rolled me to the operating room and strapped me with outstretched arms on the operating table, I experienced an immense inner peace. As I looked at all their masked faces, I recognized Dr. Prasad among them. I had not expected her to be present but felt very glad she was there. It gave me a sense of being known and well cared for. Meanwhile, I wondered how they would put me under anesthesia. I asked, and the nurse said she would give me an injection. She did, and that was the last thing I remember.

Recovery

In the days following surgery, I began to discover what it meant that I had not died and would soon recover. I had to face the simple fact that I returned to a world from which I had been released. I was glad to be alive, but on a deeper level I was confused, and I wondered why it was that Jesus had not yet called me home. Yes, I was happy to be back among friends, but still I had to ask myself why it was better for me that I return to this "vale of tears." I was deeply grateful to know that I would be able to live longer with my family and community, but I also knew that living longer on this earth would mean more struggle, more pain, more anguish, and more loneliness.

My main questions became: "Why am I alive? Why wasn't I found ready to enter into the house of God? Why was I asked to return to a place where love is so ambiguous, where peace so hard to experience, and joy so deeply hidden in sorrow?" The question came to me in many ways, and I knew that I had to grow slowly into the answer.

I realized on a very deep level that dying is the most important act of living. It involves a choice to bind others with guilt or to set them free with gratitude. This choice is a choice between a death that gives life and a death that kills. I know that many people live with the deep feeling that they have not done

It was only
in the face of death
that I clearly saw,
and perhaps only fleetingly,
what life was all about.

for those who have died what they wanted to do, and have no idea how to be healed from that lingering guilt. The dying have the unique opportunity to set free those whom they leave behind.

As I reflect on this in the light of my own encounter with death, I become aware of how unfamiliar this way of thinking is, not only for the people with whom I live and work, but also for myself. It was only in the face of death that I clearly saw — and perhaps only fleetingly — what life was all about. Intellectually, I had understood the concept of dying to self, but in the face of death itself it seemed as if I could now grasp its full meaning. When I saw how Jesus called me to let go of everything and to trust fully that by doing so my life would be fruitful for others, I could suddenly also see what my deepest vocation had always been.

My encounter with death told me something new about the meaning of my physical death and of the lifelong dying to self that must precede it.

My return into life and its many struggles means, I believe, that I am asked to proclaim the love of God in a new way. Until now I have been thinking and speaking from time into eternity, from the passing reality toward a lasting reality, from the experience of human love to the love of God. But after having touched "the other side," it seems that a new witness is called for: a witness that speaks back into the world of ambiguities from the place of unconditional love. This is such a radical change that I might find it very hard, yes even impossible, to find the words that can reach the hearts of my fellow human beings.

I know now that the words spoken to Jesus when he was baptized — "You are my Beloved" — are words spoken also to me and to all my brothers and sisters. Once I have accepted the truth that I am God's beloved child, unconditionally loved, I can be sent into the world to speak and to act as Jesus did.

The great spiritual task facing me is to so fully trust that I belong to God that I can be free in the world — free to speak even when my words are not received; free to act even when my actions are criticized, ridiculed, or considered useless; free also to receive love from people and to be grateful for all the signs of God's presence in the world.

When I awoke from my operation and realized that I was not yet in God's house but still alive in the world, I had an immediate perception of being sent: sent to make the all-embracing love of the Father known to people who hunger and thirst for love, but often look for it within a world where it cannot be found.

I understand now that "making known" is not primarily a question of words, arguments, language, and methods. What is at stake here is a way of being in the truth that tries less to persuade than to demonstrate. It is the way of witness. I must remain on the other side while being sent back. I have to live eternity while exploring the human search in time. I have to belong to God while giving myself to people.

Having touched eternity, it seems to me impossible to point toward it as though it were not already here. Jesus spoke from his intimate, unbreakable communion with the Father into the world and thus connected heaven with earth. To Nicodemus he says, "We speak of what we know, and bear witness to what we have seen" (John 3:11). Can I become like Jesus and witness to what I have seen? Yes, I can live in God and speak to the human reality. I can be at home in what is lasting and see significance in what passes away. I can dwell in the house of God and still be at home in the houses of people. Nurtured by the bread of life, I can work for justice for those who are starving to death for lack of food. I can taste the peace that is not of this world and engage myself in human struggles to establish justice and peace on earth.

There is, however, the danger of false security, of imagined clarity, yes, even of absolutism or dogmatism: the old temptation to control. Speaking from eternity into time can easily be perceived as oppressive, since answers may be offered before questions are raised. But Jesus' whole ministry was a ministry "from above," a ministry born of a relationship with the Father in heaven. All the questions Jesus raised, all the answers he gave, all

*I can dwell
in the house of God
and still be at home
in the houses of people.*

the confrontations he evoked and the consolations he offered were rooted in his knowledge of the Father's unconditional love. His ministry was not oppressive, since it came from his deep experience of being unconditionally loved and was in no way motivated by a personal need for affirmation and acceptance. He was completely free precisely because he did not belong to the world but exclusively to the Father.

For me, the question is whether my encounter with death has freed me enough from the addictions of the world that I can be true to my vocation: to live from above. It clearly involves a call to prayer, contemplation, silence, solitude, and inner detachment. I have to keep choosing my "not belonging" in order to belong, my not being from below in order to be from above. The taste of God's unconditional love quickly disappears when the addictive powers of everyday existence make their presence felt again. The clarity of the meaning of life received on a hospital bed easily fades away when the many daily obligations return and start dominating life again. It requires an enormous discipline to remain a disciple of Jesus, to continue to stay anchored in his love, and to live primarily from above. But the truth of the hospital experience cannot be denied, even though it seemed only a glimpse of the sun shining behind a cloud-covered sky. The many clouds of life can no longer fool me into denying that it is the sun that offers warmth and light. But without a very explicit and self-directed attempt to keep God in the center of my heart, it will not take long before the hospital experience becomes little more than a pious memory.

The way my friends reacted to my recovery caused me to reflect on the way life and death are perceived in our society. Unanimously, they congratulated me on my restoration to health and expressed their gratitude that I was doing so well again. Although I was deeply grateful for their attention and affection, the encounter with God in my hours near death made me wonder whether being "better again" was indeed the best thing for me. Would it not have been preferable to have been completely set free from this ambiguous world and taken home to the full communion with God?

I am discovering that Paul's dilemma — whether to honor Christ by life or by death — has become my own. The tension created by this dilemma is a tension that now lies at the basis of my life. Paul writes:

"Life to me, of course, is Christ, but then death would be a positive gain. On the other hand again, if to be alive in the body gives me an opportunity for fruitful work, I do not know for which I should choose. I am caught in this dilemma: I want to be gone and be with Christ, and this is by far the stronger desire, and yet for your sake to stay alive in this body is a more urgent need. This much I know for certain, that I shall stay and stand by you all to encourage your advance and your joy in the faith, so that my return to be among you may be ample cause to glory in Christ Jesus on my account" (Phil. 1:21–26).

I pray that these words of Paul may increasingly become my guide. Having come to realize that my death could have been a gift to others, I now know, too, that my life still to be lived is just as much a gift because both dying and living find their true meaning in the glory of Jesus Christ. Therefore, there is nothing to worry about. The risen Christ is the Lord of the living as well as the dead. To him belongs all the glory, honor, and praise. It may be that the mirror of a passing van has touched me just to remind me of that.

Epilogue

It has been five years since I wrote down my experience in the portal of death. Looking back at it now that I am again fully immersed in the complexities of daily living, I have to ask myself, "Can I hold on to what I learned?"

I have lost much of the peace and freedom that was given to me in the hospital. I regret it; I even grieve over it. Once again there are many people, many projects, many pulls. There is never enough time and space to do it all and feel totally satisfied. I am no longer as centered and focused as I was during my illness. I wish I were. I yearn for it.

However, I can no longer sit and wait for another accident to point me toward the Kingdom once again. I simply have to open my eyes to the world in which I have been placed and become then more and more who I am: a child of God. I know for sure that my accident was nothing but a simple reminder of who I am and what I am called to become.

HENRI J. M. NOUWEN, author of more than thirty books, including *The Return of the Prodigal Son, Life of the Beloved, In the Name of Jesus,* and *Our Greatest Gift,* has taught at the University of Notre Dame, Yale, and Harvard. For the last seven years, he has shared his life with people with mental handicaps, as pastor of the l'Arche Daybreak community in Toronto, Canada.

Other books in *The Path* series